AF801193

THE 11TH COMMANDMENT

THE POWER TO GET WEALTH

SIDNEY LLOYD ROBINSON

CONTENTS

ISBN: 978-1-7353694-7-1

Library of Congress Control Number: 2024922693

Cover designs by Rob Williams (C5 Designs)
Fiverr.com/cal5086

Printed by Maximalist Media Group, LLC, in the United States of America.

First printed edition 2024.

Maximalist Media Group, LLC
PO Box 1912
Eagle, ID 83616
www.maximalistmediallc.com

DEDICATIONS

To Myles, Ryley, and Corbyn—

You are my greatest inspiration and the brightest lights in my life. Everything I do, I do with you in mind, and it is my hope that this book serves as a testament to the greatness that lives within each of you. May you always know that you were born to lead, conquer, and leave a lasting impact on this world. Never be afraid to dream big, to rise above, and to take hold of the future that is yours. You have the power within you to become anything you desire, and I am endlessly proud of the incredible people you are becoming. The World is Yours!!!

I love you all to infinity and beyond,

Daddy

To my mother, Janie "J Rob" Robinson—

You are the (earthly) foundation on which my everything is built. Your unwavering love, strength, and guidance have shaped me into the man I am today, and I am forever grateful. This book is not only a reflection of my journey but of the values you instilled in me from the very beginning. Thank you for teaching me the meaning of resilience, faith, and the power of hard work. Everything I have accomplished is because of you (and God), and I dedicate this book to you with all my heart.

This one's for you, with all my love,

Sidney (aka Your Favorite Son)

PROLOGUE

THE 11TH COMMANDMENT – A DIVINE PATHWAY TO WEALTH

The 11th Commandment is not merely a book; it is an unabridged expression of divine wisdom born from revelations that took root in my childhood and blossomed throughout my life. From a young age, I embarked on a quest to understand wealth—not just through the world's definition but through spiritual truth. This fascination, sparked by curiosity and driven by purpose, ignited a relentless pursuit that has shaped the journey you are about to take with me.

I remember those early days, scouring the shelves of libraries, seeking answers, hungering for a deeper understanding of what it meant to prosper. Books like The Art of the Deal by Donald Trump, Think and

Grow Rich by Napoleon Hill, and How to Be Rich by J. Paul Getty became my companions. I soaked up their strategies, insights, and stories of success. But even as I consumed the knowledge of these men, a question lingered in my soul: What is the true source of wealth?

I knew there had to be more—something beyond mere financial strategies, beyond the accumulation of money and material possessions. There had to be a higher purpose, a divine calling embedded within the pursuit of wealth. And I found the answers I sought in the pages of Scripture, not in the halls of power. God's Word became my foundation, revealing principles that aligned with the wisdom of the ages and transcended it. I began to see wealth not as an end but a tool—a resource entrusted to us by the Creator for the greater good.

This book is the culmination of those revelations and years of studying, praying, and seeking divine wisdom on the subject of prosperity. The 11th Commandment is a thoughtful blend of biblical principles intertwined with an engaging and transformative journey toward abundance. It's not just about financial gain; it's about discovering the true meaning of wealth and how to walk in the fullness of God's promise for your life.

Within these pages, you'll find principles for becoming, growing, sustaining, and generously sharing wealth. But these principles go deeper than just financial tips. They touch the core of who you are—your identity, purpose, and God-given potential. This is a blueprint for those who refuse to settle for a life of mediocrity, for those who believe that God has called them to something greater, something impactful.

The 11th Commandment offers you more than practical advice. It offers you keys to unlock the doors of abundance—keys forged in the fire of faith and refined by the wisdom of Scripture. This is about more than just getting rich; it's about aligning yourself with God's ultimate design for your life. It's about discovering His purpose for your wealth and using it to build a legacy that will outlast you.

As you progress through these chapters, may God reveal His perfect plan for an abundant life. You will not only gain financial insights but also uncover the depth of God's master plan—a plan that empowers your quest for wealth while guiding you toward spiritual growth, leadership, and influence. The 11th Commandment will light the path to prosperity, leading you through robust spiritual and practical pathways culminating in abundance.

Let this book be your companion, your guide on this journey.

As you engage with the principles within, don't just read them—live them. Take them to heart and let them transform your thoughts about wealth, success, and purpose. God has already equipped you with everything you need to prosper, but it's up to you to step into that calling.

The pages ahead hold the blueprint to unlock the doors you've been standing before for too long. Whether you are just beginning your journey toward financial freedom or seeking a deeper understanding of how to multiply and sustain your wealth, this book will meet you where you are. It will challenge you to think bigger, dig deeper, and move forward with the confidence that God has ordained your steps.

I invite you to dive in with an open heart and mind. This is not just a roadmap for acquiring wealth—it's a call to action, a call to embrace the fullness of the life God has designed for you. The truths you will uncover within these pages have the power to change not just your financial circumstances but the entire trajectory of your life. They will equip you to step into your role as a steward of God's resources and a leader in your family, community, and sphere of influence.

As you journey through these principles, I pray that God reveals His extraordinary plan for you—a plan that will take you far beyond mere financial success and lead you into a life of purpose, impact, and abundance. Remember, wealth is not just about what you can acquire; it's about what you can give, how you can serve, and the legacy you can leave for those who come after you.

So, as we begin this journey together, know this: The world is yours. The resources of heaven are behind you, and the wisdom of the ages is at your fingertips. Now is the time to step into the fullness of God's plan for your life. Are you ready to unlock the power of The 11th Commandment?

Let's get started.

CHAPTER 1
IT WAS ALL A DREAM

> "Dreams without God are merely wishes. But when God is the author of your dreams, they have the power to transform your life and the lives of others."
>
> TONY EVANS

I remember the day as if it were yesterday; it was 1987, and we had just installed cable TV in our house. Before that day, I would sit in school listening to the other kids laugh about shows they had watched—cartoons, music videos, and the latest hit movies. I, the neighborhood nerd, often felt even more isolated during these moments. In my household, cable TV was an expensive luxury we couldn't afford. So, I'd cast a fake laugh and nod along, pretending to know what everyone was talking about. But, without fail, one of the "cool kids" would inevitably ask me about the very thing I had never seen, and just like that, my facade would crumble.

Weekends were my escape. I would visit family members who had cable TV, doing my best to absorb as much as possible. I wasn't just watching television but gathering ammunition for Monday's school conversations. I'd memorize lines and replay moments in my head, hoping to store enough dialogue to finally fit in. Yet, by the time Monday rolled around—after enduring those long, never-ending COGIC services—I had forgotten most of the punchlines I was so sure I had locked in. Back to the corner of the lunchroom I went... again.

Then there was the day my cousin Andre snuck us a descrambler, and let me tell you, it felt like we'd hit the lottery. Life had changed overnight—or so I thought. When my mother discovered it, she reacted like we had smuggled illegal contraband into the house. In a way, I suppose we had. She made it clear that not only would she throw the descrambler out, but she'd gladly let the cops lock us up and throw away the key if it came to that. Her speech about law and order scared the mess out of me. It didn't just deter me from sneaking cable—it cemented that I would never be cut out for a life of crime. Thanks, Mom. You saved me. No, seriously, you really did.

After what felt like a lifetime of begging, haggling, and manipulative negotiations, the day finally came. We had (legal) cable!!! The whole experience felt surreal.

It wasn't long after "moving on up" that I could not sleep late one night after watching WWF Saturday Night's Main Event. Adrenaline rushed through my veins (thanks, Hulk Hogan). I started skimming through channels and stumbled upon a movie that was starting: Hunk. Now, I won't bore you with the details, but in this movie, a computer nerd made a deal with the Devil to trade his life of nerdom for the life of his dreams—muscles, fancy cars, beautiful women, tons of money. As a proud member of the "nerd fraternity," I could totally relate. And that night, as I lay in bed, I remember thinking, Man, I'd make that deal in a heartbeat. I even asked myself, "How bad could Hell really be?" But, calm down, I was only ten.

The funny thing is, God must have been listening because that night, I had a dream—a dream that wasn't mere fantasy but something far more profound, something heavenly. In the stillness of my sleep, a voice came to me. It wasn't loud or booming; it was quiet, a subtle whisper: "Remember me, the Lord. It is I who have given you the power to become wealthy." The following words hit me so hard that they still send chills down my spine today: "If you serve other gods, I promise I will crush you... I will completely destroy you."

I woke up drenched in sweat, my body freezing, but my mind on fire. If I hadn't known better, I would've thought my older brother had played some prank with a bucket of water, but no—it was something much more profound. That moment changed me forever. It wasn't just a dream; it was a divine visitation, a call to something greater, far better than any deal the Devil could offer. This was a deal with God Himself, and it set me on a path that I still walk today.

That journey hasn't been without its share of confusion, surprises, and a strange mix of perplexity and clarity. It took me years to realize that the words spoken to me in that dream were also written in

Scripture. Little did I know then, but those exact words were already etched into the Bible. That discovery came later, but from the moment I woke up, I became obsessed—obsessed with hearing that voice again, obsessed with uncovering "the secret." Was it really a message from God or just an overactive imagination? I'll tell you now, despite the lyrics of DeBarge and Biggie Smalls, it wasn't "all just a dream or a simple fantasy." No, it was a promise—a divine mandate.

But there I was, a ten-year-old kid, utterly clueless about how to figure it all out. I had no idea where to begin. I didn't know I should "seek first the Kingdom of God." I was too busy stuffing my face with snacks in the church basement. Looking back, maybe I heard it, but at the time, I didn't understand that God held the answers to everything, including wealth.

Honestly, my early understanding of God and money was pretty limited. All I knew came from hearing Malachi 3:8, quoted by our head deacon every week: "Will a man rob God? Yet ye have robbed me... in tithes and offerings." The congregation sat there every Sunday, feeling the weight of those words, almost like being cursed if we didn't give enough. My thoughts on wealth and God? Let's just say they weren't very expansive. Yet, even then, something deeper was stirring. Something beyond just giving, beyond just church protocol. I just didn't know where to find it.

So, I did what most people do—searching for answers in the world. I read books like The Art of the Deal by Donald Trump, Think and Grow Rich by Napoleon Hill, and How to be Rich by J. Paul Getty. These men had amassed great fortunes, so naturally, I thought they held the answers to unlocking wealth. And yes, those books are valuable. Even now, I continue to read them, and they've certainly shaped some of my thinking. But the truth is, what God wanted to teach me couldn't be found in their pages.

Their methods didn't quite connect with the divine whisper that had rattled me to my core. It was as though I was standing at the crossroads of worldly wisdom and godly revelation, unsure of which path to follow. Little did I know that the real answers weren't locked away in the pages of self-help books—they were sitting there, in God's word, waiting to be discovered.

(Spoiler alert) I finally found that the solution to the wealth puzzle wasn't hidden in some secret formula or business strategy. It wasn't about manipulating deals or securing assets. The secret lay in God's eternal truth, in the book that had been there all along—His Word, the Bible.

As we continue this journey toward financial prosperity, it becomes clear that the Bible holds timeless principles that resonate through every aspect of economic success. Proverbs 10:4 tells us, "Diligent hands bring wealth," a truth echoed throughout history by the world's most successful people. What the world calls hard work and perseverance, God calls divine wisdom. And when you align your efforts with righteous principles, the pursuit of wealth becomes part of God's plan for your life. Wealth is not just about accumulating; it becomes about purpose, stewardship, and service.

We often fail to realize that much of the financial wisdom circulating today—whether it comes from modern-day gurus or bestselling authors—draws its inspiration from principles laid out long ago in Scripture. These aren't new ideas. The concepts of wise stewardship, sound investment, and fulfilling promises have always been central to God's teaching. Financial books are great, but the foundation of all true wealth begins with God's eternal wisdom.

Contrary to popular belief, the Bible doesn't condemn wealth—it condemns the misuse of it. Ecclesiastes 5:19 makes it plain: when God blesses someone with wealth, the ability to enjoy it with gratitude and integrity is His gift. Wealth isn't a sin; it's a tool, a resource meant to be used for good, uplifting others and expanding God's kingdom. When handled responsibly, wealth is one of the most powerful ways to make a lasting impact on the world.

And here's the thing: wealth isn't the end goal. It's a means to an end, a stepping stone to something greater. Genesis 12:2 reminds us that God blesses us so that we may be a blessing to others. Our financial prosperity is meant to spill over into the lives of those around us—improving their well-being, advancing the work of the kingdom, and ultimately fulfilling God's purpose on Earth.

So, what does all this mean? Simple: financial prosperity lies within divine wisdom. When we align our financial pursuits with biblical principles, we're not just chasing material success—we're embarking on an adventure guided by God's hand. When acquired with integrity, purpose, and gratitude, wealth becomes a tool for positive change. It becomes part of a grander narrative that extends far beyond the self and touches lives across the globe.

God didn't just give us dreams to tease us with what's possible—He gave us dreams as a call to action, as a promise of what could be if we trust Him and follow His path. The journey I embarked on as a 10-year-old boy wasn't just a personal journey toward wealth but a journey toward divine purpose. It wasn't just about becoming rich—it was about discovering what God can do through us when we align ourselves with His plan.

So, you may be asking, "What does this all mean?" Well, it was pretty simple; it wasn't just a dream. Don't get me wrong, as stated in my second book, The God Spark, this is NOT a get-rich-quick book! If that's what you were hoping for, I hate to disappoint you, but it's not that kind of party. I mean, I'm pretty creative, but I can't conjure up a way to associate the Bible with "get rich quick." So much for getting me a G650 like your favorite televangelist (or promising you one). Speaking of that, if I'm ever blessed to speak at your local church and you run to the altar throwing money at my feet, we're going viral! I'm booting you in the face like Hogan... yes, I'm still a Hulkamaniac, lol.

Anyway, now that my mother is officially embarrassed, let's move on to Chapter 2

CHAPTER 2
THE POWER

"Wealth without God is hollow, but when His power is behind it, wealth becomes a tool for changing the world."

C.S. LEWIS

Snap! You remember them, right? The song played nonstop, "The Power". You would hear it from every other car driving by, on MTV, every barbershop, and from the boombox at the basketball court. But the power I sought was more than the ability to make people dance—it was the power from my vision, The Power to Get Wealth.

Fast forward. It was the summer of 1990, and my brother and I were forced to attend Vacation Bible School. I say "forced" because we were already in church nearly every day of the week. And now we were required to go in the evening during the summer? You've gotta be kidding me! VBS felt more like jail for rich people—we knew we wouldn't be there forever and would soon get out to return to our homes. We didn't want to be there, but hey, all of my church buddies were, and there was a bonus: cookies and juice.

During a restroom break, I began flipping through a beat-up Bible, and there it was... Deuteronomy 8:18. "But thou shalt remember the Lord thy God: for it is He that giveth thee power to get wealth." I threw the Bible down and jumped. "Did I just see what I thought it said?" I picked it back up because, let's be honest, throwing down the Word of God had to be an unforgivable sin, right? (Everything else at that time seemed to be.) I continued to read the following verse: "And it shall be, if thou do at all forget the Lord thy God, and walk after other gods, and serve them, and worship them, I testify against you this day that ye shall surely perish." For the record—no, I did not make a mess of the bathroom stall! I know, too much information!

But back to that moment... there it was in print, in tangible form—the commandment from my "dream." Okay, confession time: I tore that page out. (I know what you're thinking, "He's going to burn for that one.") I don't know why. We had Bibles at home, but I did it. I read that scripture in our bathroom every night before going to bed. On that summer day, that commandment—the 11th Commandment, as I began to call it—became as clear as a burning bush or a voice on the Damascus road.

That was my awakening. I was 13 at the time. Today, I'm 47. Over the past 30-plus years, I've sought God for the steps, the secret, the formula. And I've discovered that, just like that scripture, He left the other keys in the Bible too. I would now like to share what He revealed to me with you.

THE POWER TO GET WEALTH

Wealth, in itself, is neither good nor evil. It is neutral, a tool God places in our hands to fulfill His purpose for us on this earth. Yet, in our pursuit of wealth, we often become distracted by the glitter of gold rather than the true essence of what it represents. Wealth is about stewardship. It is about being entrusted with resources to expand the Kingdom of God and bless the lives of those around us. In Deuteronomy 8:18, we are reminded: "But remember the Lord your God, for it is He who gives you the ability to produce wealth." This verse holds a powerful truth: the ability to generate wealth comes from God, but we must learn how to harness that power through obedience, faith, and action.

WEALTH AND REVERENCE OF GOD

In my early 30s, I hit a financial roadblock. No matter how much I worked or how many opportunities I chased, I felt like I was running in place. At that point, I remembered the words of Deuteronomy 8:18. I took a step back, began to meditate on what it meant to let God be the source of my provision, and sought His guidance for every decision. I learned that true wealth isn't just financial; it's holistic—encompassing family, health, and spiritual growth.

So, before we dive into the steps, let's dissect the words of this verse. To fulfill a commandment, you must first understand it clearly. First, you must remember the Lord your God. Far too often, we get caught up in the motions of life and forget about God. We forget to thank Him for life, health, and strength. We cease to give Him the honor He deserves. We spend more time keeping up with the Kardashians or debating who the GOAT is—Jordan or LeBron? (It's MJ)—than we do getting close to God. Seriously, how are you going to know more about "The Kings of Comedy" than the "King of Kings"?

The Bible makes it clear that wealth is a byproduct of wisdom. Proverbs 3:13-14 says, "Blessed is the man who finds wisdom, the man who gains understanding, for she is more profitable than silver and yields better returns than gold."Solomon, the wealthiest man to ever live, didn't start by asking for wealth—he began by asking for wisdom. He knew that wealth would be wasted without wisdom, and without God at the center, it would be meaningless.

MINDSET SHIFT TO ABUNDANCE

Wealth-building requires a shift from scarcity to abundance. Romans 12:2 reminds us to be transformed by the renewing of our minds. We often fall into the trap of thinking there's not enough to go around. But God's Kingdom operates in abundance, not scarcity. Psalms 23:1 says, "The Lord is my shepherd, I shall not want." When we truly understand this, we realize that God's provision is endless, and we begin to act in faith rather than fear.

Let's be honest: how can you remember the Lord if you don't even know who He is? If you're like me, I knew about the Lord for decades, but in hindsight, I can't say that I genuinely knew Him beyond what my pastors said during Sunday sermons. I didn't realize God wanted to be personally known until years ago. I viewed Him like the Wizard of Oz, untouchable and distant. But God doesn't want us kept at arm's length. He wants us to know Him intimately, as Adam and Eve knew Him before the fall.

To keep God at the forefront, we must surrender to Him, live for Him, and love Him. And we can't surrender unless we trust Him. We can't live for Him until we die to ourselves and follow Him. And we can't truly love Him until we know Him.

GOD IS THE SOURCE OF WEALTH

Second, remember that He gives you the power to get wealth. Now, I know what you're saying, "I'm self-made," and in the words of Drake, "I came up; it's all me." You say it's all you, huh? Really? Let's be honest. Remember COVID-19? How much power did you have then? Couldn't get to work if you tried, and I bet the stimulus check was a drop in the bucket compared to the bills piling up. You were probably praying daily for health and for God to keep your job, weren't you?

We sometimes fool ourselves into thinking we're in control, but it's God who gives us the power to become wealthy and healthy and survive each day. He is the "source of resources." Yes, you work for a company that matches your 401(k), but God's grace allows you to get up and go to that job. If God can raise kings and tear them down, as it says in Daniel 2:21, how easy would it be for Him to make all we have wither like grass?

I do not frown upon the success of individuals; if anything, I am amazed by the stories of those who have accomplished greatness. I, too, desire to add tremendous value to millions and leave an inheritance to my heirs. But I am careful not to forget that, in the end, I am allowed to be, do, and have anything—everything by God's mercy, love, and favor.

ACTIONABLE STEPS TO WEALTH

In the coming chapters, we are going to discuss the "how" of building wealth, but for a brief moment, let's break down what the 'power to get wealth' looks like in practical steps once you begin receiving it:

Stewardship: Proverbs 21:20 says, "The wise store up choice food and olive oil, but fools gulp theirs down." This teaches us the principle of saving. Set aside a portion of your income, not just for emergencies but also for investments.

Generosity: In Luke 6:38, Jesus says, "Give, and it will be given to you. A good measure, pressed down, shaken together, and running over, will be poured into your lap." Generosity is a key to unlocking God's abundance. We should be ready to give to others as part of our wealth-building strategy.

Hard Work and Diligence: Proverbs 14:23 reminds us, "All hard work brings a profit, but mere talk leads only to poverty." Wealth doesn't come by accident—it requires focused effort.

There were times when I questioned whether I had enough to even begin. But the truth is, God always gives us the seed—we just have to be willing to plant it. Galatians 6:9 encourages us: "Let us not become weary in doing good, for at the proper time we will reap a harvest if we do not give up." The power is already within you.

We are entrusted with what God gives us, and He expects us to multiply it. I think back to the parable of the talents in Matthew 25. It's a reminder that God expects us to invest the gifts He entrusted us, not bury them out of fear. You already have what you need within you. The enemy wants us to believe we're not enough and that we'll never break free from our current circumstances. But Romans 12:2 challenges us to "be transformed by the renewing of your mind."

A JEALOUS GOD

Next, remember that if you seek after "other gods, you will perish." Period. End of sentence. Your home is not your God, your kids are not your God, your career is not your God, and—sorry to disappoint—your spouse isn't either. Don't seek after other "gods." I've learned the hard way that God will "lay you out" if you do. (For those who don't have an urban dictionary on hand—or for people my mother's age—"lay you out" in this sense means "knock you out," a flat-out mental, spiritual, physical, or financial TKO!)

Though God is love, trust me, I've learned... HE IS A JEALOUS GOD! I've witnessed firsthand how swiftly God can shift things when you don't place Him first—when you "create, seek, and serve other gods." In my first book, Awaken the God Within, I shared that there was a time when I allowed my job at an investment company to become my validation. I considered myself a "mini-god" because I was thriving in my career. Newsflash! God showed me how quickly He could take it away—faster than Bounty could absorb a spill.

I had begun to seek the "god of approval" and the "god of financial worth." Guess what? Those altars I bowed before quickly disappeared, leaving me feeling emptier and more worthless than ever before. Fortunately, I serve a God of mercy and love. There's a phrase my grandmother used to say: "God loves the fool." In my case, that was true. He loved me enough not to allow me to perish. Are you as fortunate? Here's a suggestion: don't try to find out. I promise He will knock you to your knees if you don't keep Him first. If you don't make Him Lord of All, He can take it all right before your eyes.

When I state that God is a jealous God, I'm not making it up. Numerous scriptures validate the point: Exodus 20:5, 34:14, Deuteronomy 4:24, 5:9, and 6:15 are just a few. One thing they all have in common? What sparked God's jealousy was placing other gods before Him.

CONCLUSION AND ENCOURAGEMENT

The bottom line is this: Jesus replied, "Of all the commandments, which is the most important?" Jesus replied, "The most important is this: The Lord our God is the one and only Lord. And You must love the Lord your God with all of your heart, soul, mind, and strength" (Mark 12:29-30). The point I'm trying to make is that if you cannot get the MOST critical commandment (of the actual "real deal" 10 Commandments) straight by loving and keeping God first, you will never be able to live out the "11th" that I wish to share.

Now, for those of you who have a short attention span, you might be saying, "I get it, 11th Commandment, Power to Get Wealth, Don't forget God, Keep God First... yada yada yada, I got It." You may be inclined to stop reading and move on with your life, but I can assure you that knowing and application are two different things. You must know the steps to fulfill the commandment but also learn how to apply the steps to obtain wealth. Do I promise you will have overflowing financial abundance upon reading this book? Absolutely not! Contrary to what many writers (and online gurus) will say, it takes more than reading a book, completing a course, or speaking daily affirmations to make substantial amounts of money... to make any money, for that matter.

I assure you that the process and framework on which you will build your goals will be more transparent and straightforward to apply. Note: Simple is different from easy. The steps to lift weights are simple; lifting 1,000 pounds, on the other hand, is not easy. However, it is possible with wisdom, leverage, and the aid of an able team.

I get it—I have a short attention span too. I mean, why do you think I write short books? Stay with me; I promise it will be worth the wait.

CHAPTER 3
THE PRODUCE SECTION

"Create something people can't stop talking about, and you'll never have to worry about demand."

SETH GODIN

From the very beginning of time, God laid out the plan to establish wealth. Yep, it was right there initially, don't believe me? Here it goes. Genesis 1:28 KJV reads, "And God said unto them, Be fruitful and multiply, and replenish the earth and subdue it: and have dominion over the fish of the sea, and over the fowl of the air, and over every living thing that moves upon the earth. There it is for all of my fellow ADD friends: **Be Fruitful, Multiply, Replenish, and Subdue.** When you do that, you will have dominion; when you have dominion, you will create unimaginable wealth. This goes from the drug dealer on the corner to the inventor of the next must-have widget to the ruler of nations. When you do those things, you will have unlimited wealth.

LET'S START WITH THE VERY FIRST STEP: BE FRUITFUL.

I had been taught since I was a child that being fruitful meant having a bunch of children (I guess that's being fruitful and multiplying). Let me guess, you were taught that too? But if you look at it in Hebrew, fruitful meant to produce. Let me repeat it in the present tense: Fruitful Means to Produce... to come up with something. Is it not coincidental that the fruit is in the produce section when you go to the store? So, the first step to becoming wealthy is to produce something; you must create something.

It doesn't have to be something unique or brand new. The Bible says, "There is nothing new under the sun". I don't care what it is; it could be basic hamburgers or chicken sandwiches. Oh, that's funny to you? Ask In-and-Out Burger and Popeye's how funny a burger or chicken sandwich is. They (Popeye's) had people lining up for blocks to get theirs. I remember seeing video footage of people fighting over them, knocking each other out... for a chicken sandwich. Recently, in the town where I live, people camped out overnight and STILL waited for hours to have the pleasure of saying they got a burger from In-and-Out. Not laughing anymore, huh? Guess who still is? Popeyes and In-and-Out, all the way to the bank. Both are overrated, in my opinion, but they're selling like hotcakes. Perhaps I should invest in a franchise.

A CULTURE OF CONSUMPTION VS. A LIFE OF PRODUCTION

At a time when our culture seems preoccupied with acquisition and consumption, biblical wisdom holds out an extraordinary challenge: to become producers. This chapter delves into its significance. By emphasizing creation over consumption, we will uncover its transformative potential as we become better stewards of our talents and resources.

In today's society, consumption has become a lifestyle. Whether it's the constant scroll on social media or the endless pursuit of the next big purchase, the focus is on what we can get rather than give. This consumption-driven mindset leads to stagnation. It leaves people feeling unfulfilled, always chasing more but never finding satisfaction.

The Bible, however, paints an entirely different picture of fulfillment and success. Genesis 1:28, for instance, commands humanity to "be fruitful and multiply; fill the earth and subdue it." This divine directive extends beyond mere reproduction; rather, it encompasses cultivating abundance by producing goods or services to contribute to society. By adopting production roles, we align ourselves with God's divine purpose of co-creating with him. When we shift from consumers to producers, we are not just fulfilling a command but stepping into the role God designed for us—being stewards over creation. Proverbs 12:11 says, "Whoever works his land will have plenty of bread, but he who follows worthless pursuits lacks sense." This verse emphasizes the necessity of labor, diligence, and producing something meaningful.

THE BE FRUITFUL "DEEP DIVE"

Let's dive deeper into being fruitful. We often think of fruitfulness as the result of hard work, but it's more than that—it reflects who you are becoming. Producing wealth, creating value, or starting a business is not just about the outward results. It's about tapping into the creative potential God placed inside of you. Fruitfulness is a mandate that extends to every area of our lives—our relationships, work, and spiritual growth.

What does it mean to produce in your everyday life? It means taking the gifts God has given you and multiplying them. Luke 6:38 says, "Give, and it will be given to you. Good measure, pressed down, shaken together, and running over, will be put into your lap." When we give—whether it's our time, resources, or talents—God multiplies what we have in ways we can't imagine.

Remember, being fruitful is about creating something that blesses you and others. When you produce something of value—a product, a service, or even a kind word—you are sowing seeds that will eventually bring a harvest. Galatians 6:7 teaches us,

"Do not be deceived: God cannot be mocked. A man reaps what he sows." The fruit you produce today will feed you and others tomorrow.

TRANSITIONING FROM CONSUMER TO PRODUCER

Transitioning from consumers to stewards requires shifting our perspective. Jesus illustrated this point through His parable of the talents (Matthew 25:14-30), showing the significance of using and multiplying the resources entrusted to us. Faithful stewards who invested and produced were praised. At the same time, those who buried their talent faced the consequences - a powerful reminder that talents and resources are gifts that need to be nurtured, multiplied, and shared among us all.

Becoming a producer doesn't mean you must have all the answers upfront. It starts with a mindset shift. Start by asking yourself, "What has God given me that I can multiply?" This could be your skills, resources, or even your time. Every great producer began with what they had, trusting that God would multiply their efforts.

Think about the widow's oil in 2 Kings 4:1-7. All she had was a small jar of oil, but when she trusted God and acted on His instructions, that oil multiplied to meet her needs. In the same way, we have been called to take what we have, however small it may seem, and watch God multiply it as we step out in faith.

BIBLICAL EXAMPLES OF PRODUCERS

Throughout history, numerous individuals have demonstrated the concept of starting small but ultimately becoming monumentally successful through creativity and industry. Joseph is another example of this principle at work, beginning as an enslaved person but eventually becoming an influential leader through diligence, creativity, and trust in God (Genesis 39-41). Biblical examples abound, showing us the power of production over consumption. Think of Noah, tasked with producing an ark to save humanity. Moses didn't just consume God's words—he created a deliverance strategy for the Israelites that led them out of Egypt. David didn't just consume the law; he produced songs, strategies, and a kingdom that would stand for generations.

Jesus Himself was a producer. He didn't just come to teach or consume worship. He produced disciples, He multiplied bread and fish to feed thousands, and He produced a kingdom that would never fade away. As followers of Christ, we are called to the same mandate—to grow, multiply, and steward what God has placed in our hands.

Becoming a producer means more than personal success; it also involves leaving an enduring legacy. Proverbs 13:22 says, "A good person leaves an inheritance for their children's children." But that inheritance is more than just material wealth. You pass down the values, principles, and character to future generations.

Leaving a legacy is more than money; it's about producing something that will outlast you. What you create today—whether a product, a business, or even wisdom passed down—will ripple into the future.

Becoming a producer requires deliberate effort in an environment that reveres instant gratification and constant consumption. Jesus warned against materialism in Luke 12:15, warning against its allure: "Beware! Resist all forms of greed; life does not consist of an abundance of possessions." By shifting focus away from accumulating possessions toward producing value creation instead, we can escape consumer culture's grasp while moving toward living a purpose-driven existence.

Biblical wisdom underscores the call to be producers. Adopting a mindset of stewardship, creativity, and diligence aligns us with God's purpose for our lives. Examples of people who started small but achieved great success illustrate its transformative power. In an age characterized by excessive consumption, let's all heed this biblical call and become fruitful producers while fulfilling our duties as responsible stewards and co-creators with Him!

ENHANCING EXISTING IDEAS: IT'S ALL BEEN DONE BEFORE

Ok, ok, ok... so you're not a creative person. You have never thought of anything original. You can't even cook a simple meal without following instructions in a cookbook. Heck, creative for you is making a grilled cheese sandwich with three types of cheese.

Don't worry; you can still be a "producer" using things already used or done. Even Pastor Mason Betha (then Ma$e) admitted in the hit "Feels so Good" that they "take hits from the 80s, but make them sound so crazy." **I'm a born-again believer, but yeah, I still enjoy the clean/edited Bad Boy Records catalog (even after the Diddy scandal). Tell the truth, you do, too.

Ecclesiastes 1:9 reminds us, "There is nothing new under the sun." This biblical insight highlights the cyclical nature of human endeavors and reminds us that we don't need to create something entirely new to produce value. Sometimes, it's about taking something that already exists and improving it.

Elon Musk, for example, didn't invent space travel, but he innovated on it. Steve Jobs didn't invent the mobile phone; he improved how we use it.

Want something more biblically historical? Ok, here are a few... King Solomon, famed for his wisdom, set forth on an ambitious undertaking: building the Jerusalem Temple. While temples weren't exactly uncommon at that point in time, Solomon distinguished his creation through meticulous detail and innovative architectural designs he found inspiration for from skilled craftspeople of his day—creating something with greater and grander proportions than anything seen previously anywhere.

Too far in the past? Here's an "oldie but goodie."... Thomas Edison (yeah, I know, everyone always mentions him) was widely revered as one of history's great inventors and was known for relentless improvement through his inventions such as the light bulb, phonograph, and motion picture camera. These creations built upon existing ideas to further refine them—evidenced in Proverbs 14:23, which states, "All hard work yields profit while mere talking leads only to poverty."

I'm on a roll, so let's keep going... how about an illustration that's not so historical, biblical, or serious. Let me see... ok; here's a story about... a Labradoodle (yes, a Labradoodle). Ok, here it goes: Once upon a time, a cute little Poodle (let's call her Princess) was minding her business and doing what she did best: look pretty, lay in the shade, and keep her hair fluffy. One particular day, a strong, handsome Labrador Retriever was doing what he did best: retrieve a ball... mmm, maybe it was a stick. The ball/stick got into the neighbor's yard, and BOOM!!! Months later, a litter of Labradoodles was born—a literal new invention in real life.

Not long after, the Lab's dog park buddy (a scrappy Golden Retriever) met his new "puppies momma's" sister, and BOOM again... months later, Goldendoodles were born, became the next craze, and you, YES YOU lined up with money in hand to buy one for your kiddos. They probably even fought over one like it was a Popeye's Chicken sandwich. Get the point?

DON'T FORGET THE FLOWERS: GIVE CREDIT WHERE IT IS DUE

One more important thing to note is this. Pursuing improvement is admirable, yet ethical considerations must also be kept in mind. Jesus taught us to act according to the Golden Rule in Matthew 7:12: "Do unto others as you wish they did unto you." Responsible improvement involves not only expanding existing ideas but doing it in such a way that protects the well-being and rights of others. Don't be a jerk; give credit where it's due. Heck, much of this book was inspired by the teachings of my most influential virtual mentor, Pastor Myles Munroe.

CONCLUSION: THE CALL TO PRODUCE

Here's the thing: Human achievement is marked by the art of improvement. Grounded in biblical wisdom and personified by pioneers throughout history, the journey from ordinary to extraordinary unfolds through creativity, collaboration, and ethical considerations. When exploring existing ideas, we should remember our responsibility as stewards of innovation, not reinventing but rather refining existing ones to ensure their flourishing for our world's greater good.

So, ask yourself, what already exists in your world that you can take and improve upon? Perhaps you've seen a need in your community that no one addresses. Maybe you have a skill that you've been taking for granted. God has placed opportunities in your path for a reason. All you need to do is take action and start producing.

In a world obsessed with consumption, God calls us to be producers. Whether we're creating something brand new or refining an existing idea, our mandate is to contribute value to the world. The biblical examples of Noah, Paul, and Joseph, combined with modern-day entrepreneurs like Elon Musk and Sara Blakely, show us that producing is not just about wealth—it's about leaving a legacy and fulfilling our God-given purpose.

So, what will you produce?

CHAPTER 4
GREMLINS

> "To achieve massive success, you must not only duplicate your efforts but multiply them with a force that reshapes the market."
>
> GRANT CARDONE

Recently, I watched a movie from childhood that (as a youth) made me chase after every cute white and brown puppy and run scared if they got wet, all in the same moment. The movie I'm referring to was the 1980s classic "Gremlins."

I'll give you a brief summary for those who weren't born then or never saw it. In the movie, a man bought a gift for his son from a Chinatown store. The creature and his siblings (still cute as ever) had one problem—a few, actually. If they got wet, had too much light, or ate after midnight, they would transform into, well, let's say, something hideous. Worst of all, they would multiply—like roaches in a Mississippi kitchen or baby mommas after the NFL draft. Even worse, once they multiplied, they would commence destroying the town.

Why do I mention this movie? First of all, because if you haven't noticed by now, I'm a movie junkie, and second, because, just like Gremlins, if you want to make some "damage" in this world, you first have to multiply. Step two on the pathway to wealth is: **Multiply**!

Again, in Genesis 1:28, it wasn't about having a ton of children. The word multiply merely means to reproduce. So again, you need to produce something. You take an idea, develop a product or skill, and then reproduce it. How do you reproduce it? You make more of it available and find others to help reproduce it.

You could have the best idea, most incredible product, or unmatchable service in the world, but if it's sitting on a shelf and not being reproduced, you will never create wealth. How many great products and ideas are in the graveyard right now? How many ideas have you witnessed being developed and brought to market by someone else you've never met? I know I've had a few—more than I care to mention. Talk about depressing.

As discussed in chapter three, you'll find produce, such as fruit, in the produce section. That fruit will often have been reproduced by the same plants or trees. In the same way that nature reproduces more of its abundance, it is within your power to do the same. The key is finding the best way to do so with the ability to do the next step (replenish)... but more on that later.

Not to "get deep," but let me say this: sharing and multiplying what we have is of great significance in human existence. It's not simply an act of amassing wealth or knowledge for personal gain; it represents our understanding that true abundance lies in sharing it with others.

Drawn from historical and scriptural precedent, Jesus's story of multiplying fish and bread provides an unforgettable example. A meager offering miraculously became sufficient nourishment for an entire crowd. Its significance lies not only in delivering physical sustenance but in sharing and replenishing surplus supplies with those less fortunate than oneself.

As the Bible says, "Give, and it shall be given back to you; a good measure pressed down, shaken together and running over will be poured into your lap; for with the measure you use, it shall be measured back." (Luke 6:38, NIV) This principle emphasizes the reciprocal nature of sharing—multiplying returns through generosity.

HOW TO MULTIPLY WHAT YOU'VE CREATED

So, how can someone without Divine Powers of Multiplication reproduce what they've created? The idea of multiplying isn't just theoretical—it's something you can start today, step by step, with a bit of creativity and effort.

First, multiplying starts with copying what works. Whatever you've created—a product, a service, or an idea—you first need to figure out how to make more of it. You don't have to do it all yourself, either. Start thinking about how to get help, whether from others or using simple tools that make the job easier. Ask yourself: "Can someone else help me with this, or can I set it up so it works even when I'm not around?"

Let's say you've got a product. You don't have to create every single thing by hand. Maybe you can collaborate with someone better at making the product or automating some of the steps. If you have a few friends or people you know who are good at certain things, don't be afraid to ask for help. You don't need to control every little thing. Your value isn't just in doing it all yourself—it's in getting it out there for people to buy or use. You'll burn out if you try to do everything and nothing multiplies.

Now, let's say you're offering something like knowledge or a skill you've got—maybe you've written a book, started a blog, or taught a class. The key is to find ways to share what you know with more people. That's where the internet comes in handy. Platforms like Amazon, YouTube, or even social media make it easy to get what you've got in front of more people. You don't need a big team or lots of money to start sharing your stuff—use what's already out there.

Partner with others when it makes sense. If you've got a great product or idea, you might be able to team up with someone who can help get it in front of more people. This doesn't mean you have to spend a lot of money; it might just mean finding someone who knows people you don't or who's willing to sell your stuff in their store. Don't overthink it—it's about growing your reach without trying to do everything alone.

And if you offer services, the trick to multiplying is figuring out how to help more people at once. Instead of providing one-on-one services, you could create a group program, run workshops, or even record videos people can watch independently. That way, you share what you know with more people without being there every time.

HERE ARE A FEW SIMPLE WAYS TO MAKE IT HAPPEN:

Use tools that work for you: If you're selling a product, look for accessible platforms to handle the tough stuff, like printing or shipping. For example, Teespring does everything from printing your designs to shipping them. You just focus on getting people to buy. If you're sharing knowledge, platforms like Amazon or Spotify can take care of the details, letting you earn money even while you sleep.

Keep it small but scalable: You don't have to start big. Even if you're creating a few things, look for ways to make more without burning out. If you're making a product, try to find ways to create it cheaper as you make more. Consider automating small things like scheduling appointments or sending follow-up emails for services. That way, you free up more time to help more people.

Teach others: Sometimes, the best way to multiply is to teach others how to do what you do. If you're good at something, why not show someone else how to do it? That way, you can focus on the big picture while they help with the day-to-day. Plus, when others learn from you, they further spread your ideas.

Get your tribe to spread the word – Build a small community of people who love what you do. Word of mouth is powerful; the more people talk about your product or service, the more others want to try it. Social media is a great way to create these connections, but even in-person events or meetups can help get the ball rolling.

Don't be afraid of a bit of marketing – To multiply, people need to know what you've got. You don't have to spend big bucks—start with social media or even ask friends and family to share your stuff. The more eyes on your work, the more chances you have to grow.

Sell through different channels – Don't limit yourself to one place. If you've got a product, can you sell it online, in a local shop, or even at a farmer's market? If you've got knowledge, can you share it through a blog, a podcast, or a video course? The more places people can find you, the more chances they'll have to buy from you.

Finally, keep this in mind: Multiplying is all about your mindset. You have to think beyond just what you can do today. Instead of focusing on how much you can produce, ask yourself, "How can this grow without me doing everything? How can this keep going even when I'm not there?" Multiplication isn't just about quick gains—it's about building something that can last.

Multiplying isn't just about creating wealth—it's about building something bigger than yourself. When you multiply what you've produced, it touches people you've never even met. And that's how you start to create impact.

Perfect example: I have a clothing line named Resting Rich Face... yes, it's wordplay on Resting (blank) Face. I had the name and idea running through my head since I was in college, but it wasn't feasible to do anything with it in 1995. Besides, I was a broke college kid. Anyway, fast forward 25 years or so, and I finally patented the phrase, hired a few designers on Fiverr, uploaded the designs to Teespring, and finally had my own clothing line.

Sure, it's print-on-demand, not attached to a major celebrity (yet), nor is it marketed beyond word of mouth (and when I wear a shirt to the gym), but occasionally, I get a small deposit while sleeping.

I haven't even made an effort to market it. But I finally did it (create the brand) to fulfill a teenage dream and rock my stuff instead of someone else's. Realistically, I could set up an IG profile for it, give a few to some athletes, post pics of them wearing them in public, and who knows—maybe I could add to the kids' college savings or buy a rental property.

One of my best friend's wife prints shirts for family reunions, birthdays, and bridal parties. She's not making millions, but she's in business. A person I met at a Tony Robbins conference in Texas has a nutritional supply brand that he "created" through white labeling, which allowed him to retire five years earlier than planned.

Does he have a multi-million dollar lab that creates newly formulated wellness supplements? Goodness no! He didn't even work out and drank liquor like it was water. He shared how he designed a logo on Canva, trademarked it, and put it on labels of generic products shipped directly from the manufacturer. He is multiplying his product line and growing his business without creating more than a logo. Get the picture? How could you get the ball rolling? How could you multiply what you have been thinking of or the creation you've been dying to share? Still don't know what that might be? Grab a copy of The God Spark; maybe it will help you out. While you're at it, hit www.therichface.com and pick up a t-shirt. Yes, you too can be "dope like me," lol.

Replicate and share creations effortlessly online through platforms such as Amazon, which is known for global distribution and enables creators to reach wider audiences. YouTube also provides global video dissemination, allowing worldwide connectivity and creator collaboration.

Leverage platforms like Amazon to tap into global markets and other online marketplaces to expand beyond geographical limitations. I'm 99 percent sure that's how you purchased this book. I literally became an internationally published author within a matter of minutes. Do I have machines printing books or a warehouse to store them? No. Does one of my closest friends in Portugal have this book on his shelf as you read this sentence? Yep.

Digital platforms like Udemy and Skillshare offer individuals opportunities to share knowledge through courses. Musicians can distribute their tracks on Spotify, Apple Music, or other streaming services. By sharing expertise and artistic endeavors, individuals contribute to an ever-expanding pool of creativity worldwide—multiplication personified!

I get it—you don't have something that is "globally desired," or you simply don't want to deal with technology. You still have options. Many physical items are made widely accessible through local markets, retail partnerships, and distribution networks. Local businesses such as farmers' markets or boutique stores can serve as valuable resources in reaching a broader audience.

Local businesses also play a vital role in community development. Partner with neighborhood enterprises to forge relationships that benefit both parties while simultaneously improving overall well-being within your locality.

Multiplying our ideas, inventions, skills, etc., and sharing them generously with others is not simply a transactional exchange but a transformative journey. As we further explore distributing tangible goods, digital creations, and shared knowledge in the next step—replenish—let's remember this timeless wisdom: "Giving brings more happiness than receiving." (Acts 20:35, NIV).

I've been fortunate to have complete strangers tell me (via email) how words I've shared on a page blessed, impacted, or transformed their lives. The value of knowing that far exceeds the monetary exchange I ever could receive.

CHAPTER 5
THE RE-UP

> "It's not the product that creates success; it's the system behind delivering it."
>
> TONY ROBBINS

I remember going to the local record store, RBG Music, as a kid to purchase the latest Teddy Riley productions. You see, Teddy Riley was the "King of New Jack Swing," and I saw myself taking his crown one day, so I had to stay current with what he was doing. He produced so many hits that it seemed I was there fairly regularly, weekly. Unfortunately for me, RBG's didn't have the buying capacity as the larger chains, so I often found myself waiting a few days for what friends in my neighborhood affectionately called "the re-up."

Let me translate for you for those who lived a more suburban life. The "re-up" was a phrase that the dope boys used when speaking about a resupply of their product of choice. Like RBG's, they had to receive a resupply of the desired product as soon as possible. If not, the competition would win their business and; from then on, have a customer for life. That, my friends, is the third step to becoming wealthy—you must **Replenish**.

To replenish something, you must continue to make it readily available and have a distribution channel. We frown upon those who have ill-gotten success, particularly those who sell drugs. Like it or not, however, they have mastered the concepts of production, reproduction, and replenishing. They have a product (high in demand, by the way), they reproduce the product (cook, cut and bag it), and they have a distribution channel. Often, they make money while they're sleeping or incarcerated—talk about a residual income business. And to top it off, what they do is illegal, and they still pull it off. So, what's your excuse?

These “pharmaceutical entrepreneurs” often enter their trade through high-risk mentorship, learning quickly how to conduct feasibility studies in untapped markets or overcrowded competition. They conduct A/B testing, product placement, negotiation techniques, and influence. While doing all of these things, they exhibit a skill set of multitasking, delegating responsibilities, people management, and word-of-mouth referrals/advertising. And you say you can’t compete with the current YouTube sensation?

The very individuals society often looks down upon are masters of marketing, eliminators of competition, and quite frequently proficient business developers, creating multiple streams of income by establishing legitimate businesses. You know what I’m talking about—the barbershop, car wash, music store, etc. Back to the topic at hand, though—just like the previous concept (reproduction), if you don’t establish a method to continuously provide your product or service to the marketplace, you will find it virtually impossible to achieve sustainable wealth.

I do not participate in MLM "business opportunities,” but I can applaud the systems they establish to build distribution chains. Pick any of them—from lotions to pills to potions—they have someone, as we speak, who is on the lookout to recruit new "distributors" that will gleefully purchase and promote to all of their family and friends. Unfortunately, 99% fail, but there will be another person waiting in the wings to continue the process. Quite often, those who didn't make it soon move on to another company and start (what I call the cycle of insanity) all over again.

Many people join these programs, and they tell people, "We're in the introductory stages of this industry" and "We haven't reached critical mass." Many of these companies target the Baby Boomer population and lament the statistics: "There are ten million baby boomers per day retiring," etc. They have various products, reproduce them, and say, "We want you to distribute and replenish it."

REPLENISHING WHAT YOU HAVE:

Let's break down how you can apply this replenishment concept to your own business or service. You don't need a huge company or an MLM-style model to make this work. It all starts with ensuring you have a system to keep your product or service in stock and available. Here are a few practical steps you can take to replenish what you offer:

Keep track of demand – First and foremost, pay attention to what people want from you. If your product or service is in demand, make sure you know how often people buy it and how quickly it moves. Don't wait until your shelves (or virtual shelves) are empty before restocking. Whether selling physical goods or offering a service, you need to know how much to keep ready to go.

Set up a simple restocking system: You don't need to get fancy immediately. Just have a way to keep track of your inventory or schedule availability. If you're selling products, make sure you have a supplier or a way to get more when needed. If you're offering a service, create a schedule that allows for a consistent flow of customers without burning yourself out. It's about being ready to meet the need when it arises.

Build relationships with suppliers: No one builds wealth alone. You need a strong relationship with those who provide you with the materials or tools to create your product. Whether it's a vendor, a manufacturer, or even a digital tool you use to run your service, maintaining a solid relationship ensures you can continually replenish when necessary.

Look at local opportunities: Like the neighborhood "pharmacist," you don't have to go far to start distributing. Think about the people around you who might be interested in what you're offering. Local groups, events, or even your network of friends and family can help you begin spreading the word. Remember, your distribution channel doesn't have to be global right away—start where you are.

The importance of continuously renewing our stocks of goods, ideas, talents, and services cannot be overstated. This renewal cycle is a pragmatic necessity and a source of enduring prosperity and growth. To contribute meaningfully to the marketplace, you must embrace abundant replenishment—meeting needs, surpassing them, and doing it all with a spirit of generosity.

Let's consider a simple example: the local artisan who passionately crafts unique goods. By constantly refining their craft and introducing new designs, they replenish the market with products and raise their industry's standards. The same can apply to whatever you create or offer. The more you refine your work and provide something fresh, the more you contribute and the more demand you create.

Those who share knowledge or expertise also embody the idea of replenishment. By freely sharing what they know, they help others and create a cycle where new ideas and innovations can flourish. The more you give, the more you get back in the form of fresh opportunities, new perspectives, and growth in your field.

Let me give you another example from my own life. A year before writing this book, I started a podcast entitled Flawed Men of Faith from the comfort of my home. I didn't have a fancy setup—just a cheap USB mic and iPad. I added some cheesy background music and recorded what I had to say. But here's the amazing part—when I uploaded the first episode to Spotify, I shared it on platforms like Apple, iHeart, and Amazon, all for free! I was able to reach a global audience without spending a dime. If I want, I can keep replenishing my listener base daily by creating more episodes and continuously feeding the audience. That's the power of replenishment.

The principle of replenishment extends beyond products and services. It's about renewing relationships, revitalizing communities, and constantly injecting life into your surroundings. Whether it's in business, your personal life, or your community, you need to think about how you can keep giving and how you can keep refreshing what you have to offer.

So, what about you? What's your distribution channel? Who could benefit from what you're offering right now? Maybe it's as simple as emailing a friend who's active in your church or fraternity. Perhaps you can advertise on social media or in the local high school sports program. The possibilities are endless, but the key is simple: start where you are.

Too often, we miss opportunities right before us because we're too focused on chasing something more significant. But here's something to consider: your neighborhood street pharmacist doesn't usually move much farther than the corner or leave their front porch. Yet, they've created an empire by focusing on what's right in front of them.

Lastly, make sure what you offer is excellent. People don't want inferior products or services—they want something that's high-quality and worth their time. Excellence speaks for itself and is one of the critical factors in replenishment.

For the record, regarding the drug dealers I mentioned earlier in this chapter—**I am in no way glorifying individuals who contribute to the destruction of families, the decay of our communities, or the toxic products they sell.** My point is simple: they understand certain principles from which we can all learn. They're fruitful (even if it's poisonous fruit), they multiply and replenish, and the next step they master is subduing.

But before we dive into that next step, let's talk more about sustaining what you've built. You see, replenishment isn't a "one and done" process—you have to do it consistently, day in and day out. This is the part of wealth-building that often gets overlooked. People are quick to talk about creating something or multiplying it, but sustaining and replenishing? That takes discipline and intention.

Look at any successful business or entrepreneur. They don't just hit the jackpot once and walk away.

They stay in the game. They continually reinvest their time, energy, and resources to ensure what they've created continues to grow. That's the beauty of replenishment. It's not just about producing more —it's about nurturing what you've built, making sure it's not only surviving but thriving in the long run.

Think about it like this: when farmers plant crops, they don't just scatter the seeds and walk away. They water, they weed, they fertilize. They maintain the soil. They're constantly replenishing the nutrients in the ground to ensure a good harvest, not just this season but for years to come. The same principle applies to you and whatever you're working on. You need to keep tending to it, refreshing it, and making sure it stays relevant.

And let's be honest for a moment. This part of the journey isn't always glamorous. Replenishment can feel repetitive, maybe even mundane at times. But this is where success is genuinely made—in the moments when you keep going, even when it doesn't feel exciting anymore. When you keep showing up, make sure your product or service is the best it can be, and constantly put in the work to stay consistent. It's in these moments of replenishment that you lay the foundation for sustainable wealth.

Now, let's not confuse this with overworking yourself. The goal here is balance—knowing when to step in and nurture and when to step back and let the systems you've put in place do the work for you. Replenishment is not about burning out but about being intentional about maintaining and growing what you've created.

Here's another thing to consider: diversification. Don't be afraid to introduce new elements when replenishing what you offer. Whether it's a fresh twist on your product, a new feature for your service, or a different way to reach your audience—constantly evolving and diversifying is another way to ensure longevity. People want something that grows with them and feels like it's continuously improving. By continually replenishing, you keep things exciting and prevent stagnation.

If you're running a business, this could mean adding a new product line. If you're in the service industry, maybe it's time to offer a premium package or expand into new areas. Whatever it is, keep the momentum going by finding new ways to add value to what you already have. Replenishment isn't just about keeping up—it's about staying ahead.

And here's the part where faith comes in. Replenishing what you've been given is also an act of stewardship. The Bible tells us to be faithful to what we've been entrusted with. That means we have a responsibility to not only protect what we've built but to grow it, nurture it, and multiply it for the greater good. When replenishing, we're not just thinking about our success—we're thinking about the people we serve, the lives we impact, and the legacy we leave behind.

So, before we move on to the following principle, I want you to think about where you are right now. What do you need to replenish in your life or business? Where have you stopped tending to your garden, so to speak? Maybe it's your time, your energy, or your resources. Maybe it's your relationships, your health, or your spiritual growth. Replenishment is about more than just money—it's about refreshing every area of your life so that you can continue to give your best, not just for today but for the future.

Take some time today to evaluate where you are. Look at your business, your personal life, and your goals. Ask yourself: "What needs to be replenished right now?" It could be a small thing or a significant shift, but whatever it is, make a plan to address it. Don't let the well run dry—be proactive and make sure you're constantly refueling.

When we truly understand and embrace the power of replenishment, we set ourselves up for long-term success. We're no longer just creating for today—we're building something that will last and stand the test of time and leave a legacy for generations to come.

With that in mind, we're ready to tackle the next step: **Subdue**. Once you've created, multiplied, and replenished, it's time to take charge. It's time to dominate your space, establish yourself as a leader, and subdue the opportunities in front of you. But before we dive into that, make sure you've laid the groundwork by replenishing what you've already built. Only then will you be ready to take the next step with confidence.

CHAPTER 6
THE ART OF SUBDUCTION

"You don't dominate the market by following the rules, but by rewriting them."

PETER THIEL

Yes, I spelled that correctly: Subduction, not seduction. I mean, come on, this is a "faith-based" book... get your mind out of the gutter, lol. What is subduction? Technically speaking, subduction is the tectonic process at convergent margins by which slabs of oceanic lithosphere descend into the mantle. (I told you I was a nerd as a kid.) In layperson's terms, it's where two plates of the earth cross paths, and one pushes down the other.

Honestly, I wrote the "smart guy definition" first because my wife graduated from Stanford, and I wanted to impress her (fingers crossed).

Anyway, what does subduction have to do with the topic of money? Nothing at all. It correlates with the fourth step in the "profit process": Subdue the earth. You see, just like that part of the earth controls and puts pressure on the other that crosses its path; you need to "control the land" which you desire to dwell within and upon. You must begin to pressure the area in which you seek to establish your success.

Who controls the industry that you are in? Who is the person in your area that people speak about when discussing what you have to offer? The very definition of subduing is to overcome or bring under control. Do you control the terms of your product or service? Do you pay others for the profits you generate or wait for others to pay you?

In the 1984 movie Dune, there was a line that stated, "He who controls the spice controls the universe." Well, in business, "he who controls the money controls you." When you subdue the competing marketplace, you will control the wealth, even if you're not issuing the checks.

While we're on the topic of the control of wealth, let me ask you, what images come to your mind? What phrases do you think about? Do you think about "the love of money is the root of all evil"? Do you think about a person working rabidly from sun up to sun down because they have to maintain material possessions as if money controls them? Are you thinking about a person who makes amoral decisions because they have become a slave to wealth? Is that the image that comes to mind?

If that is the case, your view of wealth will make it difficult to obtain. You see, anything you think negatively about will avoid you (or you will subconsciously avoid it). While in pursuit of wealth and success, one often underestimates the impact that mindset plays.

A person's belief system regarding money can either bring prosperity into their life or keep it away, creating an all-or-nothing scenario. This chapter investigates the idea that wealth eludes those with opposing beliefs regarding it.

A customer named Chelsea used to come to a bank I worked at. She was an entrepreneur with fresh ideas and an impeccable work ethic. As positive as she was, Chelsea had deeply held negative attitudes about wealth as being associated with corruption and moral compromise.

Despite working hard and having great business ideas, her financial success eluded her, as her mindset served as an invisible roadblock that prevented forward movement in her progress. She eventually went to a conference by a well-known "guru" and began networking with like-minded people in attendance; over time, her viewpoint and business bank account changed.

An old colleague, Bryan, was an ambitious professional with dreams of financial independence who continually struggled to amass wealth. Unbeknownst to him, his fundamental belief that money caused more problems than solutions stood as a blockage to success; perhaps as an outcome, prosperity always seemed out of his reach.

The crazy part is that as soon as he changed his circle of friends and began spending time with people outside of his comfort zone and "environment," his mindset changed. What happened next? Opportunities began to surface, leading him to insane amounts of success and financial reward.

Though it took time and a focused desire to change, these examples demonstrate the incredible power of one's mind in shaping financial success. It's not simply actions but thoughts that are important. Though considered a New Age concept, an increasingly popular theory within psychology and personal development, known as The Law of Attraction, posits that like attracts like. As a Christian, I support the Proverbs 23:7 scripture: "As a man thinketh in his heart, so is he.” Within wealth management terms, this equates to a positive mindset attracting prosperity while negativity repels it. Make sense now? And YES, the Law of Attraction is a copycat Biblical principle.

To escape the mindset trap, you must adjust your perspectives about money. Instead of viewing wealth as inherently corruptive, view it as an asset with which one can affect positive changes personally and in society. Adopting an abundance-minded outlook on wealth accumulation allows you to open yourself up to all this wealth brings you.

Okay, enough about money mindsets—back to the subduing. When you begin to take steps to control your piece of the market, that's when you indeed start to subdue. It's not about brute force or unethical practices but about positioning yourself so that your presence in the marketplace cannot be ignored. Think of it like a game of chess—you're not trying to eliminate the competition by sheer aggression; instead, you're strategically placing yourself in positions where your value, product, or service is indispensable. Subduing the market means understanding the landscape so well that you know the moves to make to establish dominance.

STEPS TO SUBDUE YOUR MARKET

Know Your Industry Inside Out

The first step in subduing your market is to master the ins and outs of your industry. Who are the key players? What are the trends? What are the pain points that customers are facing, and how can you solve them better than anyone else? You have to become the go-to person for the solution you provide. Read, study, and engage with industry experts. Absorb everything, and use it to your advantage. Knowledge isn't just power—it's leverage.

Become Synonymous with Your Offering

When people think of your service or product, they should think of you first. This is about brand association. It's not just about having a good product; it's about becoming the face of that product in your community or niche. How do you do this? Visibility. Start by creating value in spaces where your audience exists—through content creation, social media, or speaking at events. Establish yourself as the expert, and do it consistently.

Build Relationships, Not Transactions

One way to subdue the marketplace is by building deep, meaningful relationships with your customers or clients. You're not just selling a product or service but building trust. When people trust you, they'll come to you for your expertise, and that's a powerful position to be in. Make it a point to connect on a personal level. Be available. Follow up. Genuinely care about their success. When you build strong relationships, your competition doesn't stand a chance because your customers won't even consider going elsewhere.

Offer Something Unique

This is crucial. You can't subdue the market if you offer the same thing as everyone else. What sets you apart? What's your unique selling point? It could be something as simple as how you deliver your service or a feature of your product that no one else offers. Find what makes you different and amplify it. It could be your customer service, values, or pricing model—whatever it is, make it known that no one else does it like you do.

Control the Narrative

In any industry, the one who controls the narrative controls the perception. This means you have to stay ahead of what people say about you, your product, and your industry. Use testimonials, reviews, and social proof to back up your claims. If a negative perception forms, tackle it head-on. Don't let anyone else define what you do or who you are. Be the voice that shapes the conversation in your favor.

Leverage Technology and Trends

Technology is a game-changer when it comes to subduing the marketplace. You're already behind if you're not leveraging the latest tools and trends. Whether automating your customer service, using social media algorithms to reach a larger audience, or employing data analytics to better understand customer behavior, you must be ahead of the curve. Being technologically savvy gives you an edge and positions you as a forward-thinking leader in your space.

Invest in Yourself and Your Team

You can't dominate an industry without continuously improving yourself and the people around you. Attend seminars, invest in courses, and push your team to do the same. Personal growth and development will always translate into professional growth. The more skilled, knowledgeable, and efficient you are, the more ground you'll gain in the marketplace.

Consistency is Key

None of this works if you aren't consistent. Subduing the marketplace is about showing up daily, even when it's tough. Consistency builds reputation. Reputation builds trust. And trust leads to market dominance. The more reliable and consistent you are in delivering your product or service, the more you will become the uncontested leader in your field. Don't underestimate the power of just showing up and doing what you said you would do—time and time again.

SUBDUING ISN'T AGGRESSION—IT'S STRATEGY

Many people hear the word "subdue" and think it means using force or being overly aggressive in the marketplace. But that's not what it's about. Subduing is strategic. It's about positioning yourself so your competition has no choice but to respect and recognize your place in the industry. It's about creating so much value, delivering such high-quality work, and maintaining such a strong presence that others can't help but acknowledge your authority in the space.

It's also about longevity. Subduing means you're not just a flash in the pan—you're here to stay. You've built something that can withstand trends, competition, and market changes based on solid foundations: knowledge, relationships, consistency, and value. When you subdue your market, you build a legacy that will outlast any product, service, or campaign.

BALANCING FAITH AND BUSINESS

As a Christian, it's essential to remember that subduing the marketplace doesn't mean compromising your values. It means standing firm in your faith while being bold in your pursuits. There's nothing wrong with wanting to own your space in the business world. In fact, God calls us to dominate and take dominion over the earth. That includes the marketplace. Just like in the parable of the talents, we are expected to multiply and make the most of what we've been given. Subduing the market is simply using our gifts, resources, and wisdom to their fullest potential.

So, how do you balance ambition with faith? By making sure that everything you do aligns with your values. Ensuring that your pursuit of success is not about stepping on others but lifting them up. By understanding that true power in the marketplace isn't about greed—it's about stewardship. When you operate from a place of integrity, you're not just subduing the market—you're transforming it.

At the end of the day, subduing the marketplace is all about taking control of your space. You can't wait for others to permit you to succeed. You have to create that success for yourself. You have to believe that you can own your industry, control the narrative, and bring others under your influence. This isn't just about making money—it's about creating impact and leaving a legacy.

The marketplace is vast, and there's plenty of room for you to carve out your place. But to do that, you have to step up and take ownership of your space. You can't wait for others to recognize your value—you must show them. You have to subdue.

And once you've done that, you're not just surviving in your industry—you're thriving. You're setting the standard, and others are looking to you for direction. That's what it means to subdue the marketplace. That's what it means to own your space.

Now, it's time to go out there and take control. The world is waiting for what you have to offer. It's time to subdue.

CHAPTER 7
YOUR DOMAIN NAME

> "You were born to stand out, to rule over your domain with authority, not because of what you have, but because of who you are."
>
> ANONYMOUS

Quick question for you: What is your domain name? Some of you might be thinking, "A domain name? I don't have a business; I don't need a domain name." But that's not what I'm talking about. I'm asking, what is the area in your life you were purposed to have dominion over? Where are you designed to dominate? What is the name of that space—the name of that domain?

Each of us has a purpose in this world, but I think that, especially in Western civilization, we've convinced ourselves that our purpose must be something grand, world-changing. We've told ourselves that it's only valid if it's noteworthy if it's on the level of the titans of this world. But that mindset is flawed.

The core of your purpose may not affect anyone outside of your neighborhood, city, or even the walls of your home, but that does not diminish its importance. It is still your domain, the space you were created to dominate and have authority over. So again, I ask you: What is your domain name? What were you created to do? Who were you made to be?

Once you identify what that is, you can define your domain name and walk in with the power of knowing your true purpose. But far too often, we see people doing something that resonates within us, and we begin to think, "Maybe I can do that too." We start to take on someone else's purpose and dominion and wonder why we don't accomplish anything meaningful. The truth is we were all created by God to have dominion in a specific area. That dominion might be within your local family business or on a global platform—but whatever it is, you were created to own it.

You can't compare your purpose to someone else's. We end up in an identity crisis when we fall into that trap. I'm sure you've experienced it—when you find yourself trying to fit into someone else's shoes, even though they don't quite fit. Remember the era when everyone wanted to "be like Mike"? Kids and adults alike were trying to emulate Michael Jordan on the court. But no matter how many people stuck their tongues out or wore unneeded knee braces, they would never be Michael Jordan. Why? Because they weren't created to be him. They were trying to live in someone else's dominion instead of discovering their own.

For me, growing up, it wasn't about being like Mike. Aside from my older cousin Derrick (mentioned in one of my previous books), I wanted to be like Babyface and (again) Teddy Riley—producing chart-topping music, owning my record label, and working with stars worldwide. I even tried to look like them! But no matter what I did, I could never authentically be myself while trying to be someone else. It wasn't until I embraced who I was that I could step into my own dominion.

LIVING OUT YOUR IDENTITY

There's nothing wrong with being inspired by others. In fact, we all do it. Our children often act like us, and we carry ourselves similarly to our parents or mentors. It's called mirroring, and it's as natural as breathing. But here's the key: when it comes to purpose, you have to live out your own identity.

You must discover and define who you are. You weren't cut out to be someone else. Ask yourself: Who am I? What is my domain name? Where were you created to reign? What rhythm does your heart naturally beat to? What lane do you move in without effort?

If you don't know, ask the people around you. I'm cautious about this advice because sometimes people can't see their potential and struggle to recognize yours. Others might try to limit you, placing you in a box that's easy for them to understand and manage. But if you hear eight out of ten people saying the same thing about you, maybe they're onto something. That could be a clue to discovering your domain.

But don't stop there. Once you've got a sense of what your domain might be, take action. Far too many people spend their lives waiting for their purpose to be revealed as if God will send them a lightning bolt moment while they're sitting on the couch. Purpose doesn't work that way. You discover your domain as you move forward—one step at a time. Start small. Begin exploring what it feels like to operate in your gift. Take a class. Start a project. Volunteer in an area that resonates with you. You won't know if you've found your domain until you engage with it.

Dominion Directive 1: Start Where You Are

The key is to start where you are. You don't need to wait until you have everything figured out. God is more concerned with your willingness than your readiness. As you take steps of faith, your domain will start to come into focus. It might take time, but doing something is the only way to get clarity. So ask yourself right now: What is one thing I can do today to explore my domain? Maybe it's starting a blog to share your insights. Perhaps it's volunteering in a local ministry to see if that's your calling. Maybe it's something as simple as writing down the things that naturally energize you. Whatever it is, take that step.

Dominion Directive 2: Define Your Unique Offering

Now that you've started, you need to define what makes your domain unique. This is where you begin to refine your gift. God didn't create you to be a copy of someone else. What is the unique twist or approach you bring to your space? It could be your personality, experiences, or how you deliver value. Think about it—no one can offer what you offer in the way you do. When you find that, amplify it. Let that be the foundation of your dominion.

Dominion Directive 3: Develop Your Domain

Once you've identified your domain, the next step is to develop it. This is where the real work begins. You have to commit to growing in your area of expertise. Remember, having dominion doesn't mean you've arrived. It means you're constantly growing, learning, and evolving within your space. That's how you dominate—by becoming the best version of yourself in that domain.

For example, if you discover your domain is leadership, start studying great leaders. Learn from their successes and their failures. If your domain is teaching, become the best educator you can be. If your domain is entrepreneurship, immerse yourself in the business world. Master your craft. The more you invest in developing your domain, the more authority you gain. People will start looking to you as the expert, as the go-to person in that space. That's when you know you've begun to dominate.

Dominion Directive 4: Build a Tribe

One of the most critical aspects of dominion is influence. And influence doesn't happen in a vacuum. To dominate your domain, you need to build a tribe. These are the people who are inspired by what you do, who are impacted by your gift, and who spread the word about your work. You can't be a leader if no one is following. The more you pour into others, the more your tribe will grow. And as your tribe grows, so does your dominion.

How do you build a tribe? By adding value. Give people a reason to follow you. Share your knowledge, your insight, and your time. Create a community where people feel connected to your mission. Whether through social media, a business, or simply the relationships you build in your neighborhood, influence starts with service. The more you serve, the more you'll attract the people who will support you in your journey.

Dominion Directive 5: Own Your Domain

Here's where we get to the heart of dominion: ownership. Once you've identified, developed, and built your tribe within your domain, you have to own it. This means taking responsibility for the space God has entrusted to you. You can't dominate something you aren't willing to take responsibility for. If your domain is within your family, be the leader your family needs. If your domain is in business, make sure your business reflects the values and excellence you believe in. Ownership means stepping fully into the role God has given you.

But ownership also means dealing with the tough stuff. There will be challenges, competition, and setbacks. But when you own your domain, you don't back down when things get complicated. You lean into the challenges, knowing God has given you everything you need to succeed. You were created to thrive, not just survive.

THE POWER TO DOMINATE

Let me ask you one last time: What is your domain name?

The answer to this question isn't just a fun thought exercise—it's the key to unlocking everything I've shared throughout this book. You were created to have dominion. You were equipped to succeed. God has placed unique gifts inside of you, and now is the time to use them.

The Bible tells us in Genesis 1:28 that we are to be fruitful, multiply, and have dominion over the earth. It doesn't say that dominion is reserved for the elite few—it says that you are called to dominate. But that doesn't always mean you have to conquer the world. It might mean you need to dominate in your community, your industry, or even your household.

Your influence might be regional, local, or even personal—but it's yours to own.

Don't be discouraged if your dominion isn't on a global scale. Start small. Start where you are. God has entrusted you with an area to rule over, and as you steward that domain faithfully, He will expand your territory. Faithfulness in the small things leads to more incredible things.

THE TIME IS NOW

There's no time left to delay. You have everything you need to step into your purpose and dominate your domain. You've read the previous chapters and learned how to produce, reproduce, replenish, and subdue. Now, it's time to take dominion.

Don't wait for the perfect moment. Don't wait until you feel "ready." The truth is, you're never going to feel fully prepared. But God doesn't call the qualified —He qualifies the called. And if you're reading this, you are called to something greater.

Step boldly into your purpose. Don't shy away from the responsibility of owning your domain. Whether it's local, regional, or global, your dominion matters.

The world needs what you have to offer, and people are waiting for you to step up and serve in the way only you can.

This is your time. This is your moment. You have the power to get wealth, and now you know how to use it. Honor God with your gifts. Be a blessing to those around you. And dominate the domain He has entrusted to you.

As you do, you'll fulfill your purpose and experience the joy, fulfillment, and abundance of walking in alignment with God's will.

So, I ask you once again: What is your domain name?

CHAPTER 8

THE WORLD IS YOURS

> "The world is yours and everything in it, it's out there, get on your grind and get it"
>
> NAS

Remember that iconic scene from Scarface when Tony Montana is standing in Frank's waterfront mansion, staring out the window? A blimp drifts across the night sky, illuminating with the words: "The World is Yours." At that moment, Tony's hunger for power, wealth, and success is encapsulated in those four words. Though his path was far from righteous, the idea behind that phrase is undeniable—the world is full of opportunities, and it's up to you to take hold of them.

Unlike Tony Montana, we're not here to chase riches through questionable means. We're here to build wealth the right way, honoring God in the process. But the message remains: The world is yours. What will you do with it?

You've made it to the end, but let me tell you something—this is just the beginning.

By now, you've taken a deep dive into what it means to walk in dominion. You've learned how to produce, reproduce, replenish, and subdue. You've been given the tools to change your financial situation and life. You've been shown that wealth is not just about money—it's about purpose, gifting, and impact. But here's the real deal: none of this matters if you don't take action.

I've walked with you through every chapter, laid out the blueprint, shared the principles, and connected them to God's design for your life. But now, the rest is on you. The power to get wealth has already been given to you (Deut. 8:18). The question is, what will you do with it?

Let's take a moment to recap the journey you've just been on.

REWIND TO THE BASICS: PRODUCING, MULTIPLYING, REPLENISHING, SUBDUING

We started by discussing producing—you can't multiply what you haven't produced. If you've read this book and haven't identified the gifts, skills, or ideas God has placed in you, now is the time. You have something only you can offer to this world, and if you're not producing, you're not fulfilling the purpose God designed you for.

Next, we talked about multiplying what you've produced. One product, one skill, and one idea is not enough. In God's economy, He doesn't just want you to add; He wants you to multiply. Multiply your gifts, opportunities, and income streams—reproduce what's been given to you so you can touch more lives, build wealth, and have a greater impact.

Then came the critical step: replenishing. The key to lasting success isn't just about making it big one time. It's about sustainability. You've learned how to keep your storehouses full and have a system that replenishes what you've produced so that you're always ready to give, serve, and grow.

Finally, we discussed subduing—the moment you take control of your domain. You're not just existing in your industry, family, or community—you're dominating it. You're setting the tone, establishing authority, and living in the fullness of the power God has given you.

Each of these steps has been more than just a roadmap to wealth—it's been a guide to living in your purpose, walking in abundance, and creating a life that glorifies God while blessing others.

THE MISSING PIECE: OWNERSHIP

But there's one final thing that connects this all, and I want to leave you with it as we close out this book: **Ownership**.

You see, you can have all the tools in the world, but until you own the responsibility for your future, none of it will matter. It's not enough to know you have a gift. It's not enough to know the steps to get wealth. You have to own your role in this process. You must claim your authority in the space God has given you and walk in it without fear or hesitation.

So many people get stuck at the point of knowing. They know what to do, what they're capable of, and even know they're called to greatness—but they never move. Why? Because ownership comes with responsibility. It means you can no longer wait for someone else to give you permission. You have to give yourself permission to step into the life God has already promised you.

DOMINION REQUIRES DISCIPLINE

I'm going to keep it real with you: this journey isn't easy. Dominion doesn't happen overnight. It requires discipline, sacrifice, and persistence. You're going to face setbacks. There will be moments where you doubt yourself, the opposition seems too strong, and you feel like giving up. But let me remind you: you are equipped for this. God doesn't bring you to the battlefield without giving you the tools to win the fight.

Wealth isn't for the faint of heart. It's for the warriors, the builders, who aren't afraid to get their hands dirty and put in the work. So, ask yourself: Are you ready to own your domain? Are you ready to take dominion?

The Next Step: It's Time to Move

Now that you've walked this far, it's time to take the next step. This is where you put everything you've learned into action. Don't let the principles in this book sit on a shelf. Don't be the person who gains knowledge but never applies it. Apply what you've learned, and watch your life transform.

Here's what I want you to do next: Own Your Gifts

Go back to the chapter on producing. Identify what it is that God has placed inside of you. Is it a skill, a talent, a product, or an idea? Whatever it is, own it. Stop waiting for the "right moment" to use your gift. Now is the right moment.

Multiply What You Have

Take what you've been given and multiply it. If you've already started a business, think about how you can expand it. If you've been developing a skill, think about how you can leverage it to reach more people. Do more with what you have.

Create Systems to Replenish

Make sure you have a system in place to keep things moving. Whether it's in your finances, business, or relationships—develop processes that keep you full, so you're never operating from a place of lack.

Take Control of Your Domain

Stop waiting for someone to hand you the keys. Subdue your marketplace, your community, and your industry. You don't need permission to walk in your calling. Take control of the space God has given you.

LET'S STAY CONNECTED

Now, before we close, I want you to know that this journey doesn't have to end here. You've read the book, but that doesn't mean we have to part ways. I want to connect with you. Let me know how this book has impacted your life, what steps you're taking, and what areas you're walking in dominion.

You can reach me directly through my website at www.sidneyondemand.com. I'm also on social media—find me on Facebook and Instagram (@sidneyondemand) and share your story. I want to hear about the moves you're making and the victories you're walking in.

And, more importantly, share what you've learned with others. Someone in your circle needs to hear this message and is waiting for the encouragement to step into their domain. Don't keep this to yourself. Spread the word, and let's build a community of people ready to dominate their space, create wealth, and honor God.

THE FINAL WORD: IT'S YOURS NOW

This book was never just about the steps to wealth. It's about discovering your true calling, walking in your God-given authority, and using the resources you've been blessed with to make a difference. I've shared everything I know with you. I've given you the keys. Now it's your turn.

Take the principles you've learned. Walk in your purpose. Step into your dominion. And remember, wealth is not just about money—it's about who you become in the process.

You were created for greatness. You have the power to acquire wealth, and you have the responsibility to use it wisely.

So go out there. Own it. And let the world see what happens when you walk in the fullness of what God has for you.

In closing, I once heard a quote by an unknown source that said, "The world is yours. Own it. Take the next step as if you were meant to dominate."

So yes, my friend, The world IS yours indeed.... Well, technically, it's "Our Fathers."

What will you do with it?

THE BONUS CHAPTER

FROM BILLS TO BILLIONS

> "The question isn't who is going to let me; it's who is going to stop me."
>
> AYN RAND

Surprise! Just like your favorite Jodeci album, this book wouldn't be complete without a hidden bonus track. If you've read my first two books, Awaken the God Within and The God Spark, you already know I'm a fan of throwing in something extra, inspired by the kings of R&B who always gave us that secret gem at the end of the album. Well, I couldn't break tradition, could I?

This chapter is your bonus track. Just like when Jodeci hit you with those smooth, unexpected songs, this chapter is here to make sure you leave on a high note, motivated, inspired, and ready to move.

Since the title of this Bonus Chapter has the words "Bills" and "Billions," let's talk about another "Bill", Bill Gates. So, "Uncle Bill," as I call him (maybe he'll find out and leave me in the will), didn't just create a product- he created dominion. He saw a need and filled it. He didn't stop at creating something cool—he multiplied, reproduced, and made it so essential that Microsoft was everywhere. It didn't just live on one computer but on every computer.

But before Uncle Bill became the global tech icon we know today, he was just another guy with an idea. He started in his garage, much like any ordinary person with a vision. He didn't have legions of employees or unlimited resources. He had a product, a dream, and a relentless belief that he could change the world. His story is the perfect reminder that the seeds of greatness are often planted in the most humble beginnings. And when you nurture those seeds with consistent action, they grow into something much bigger than you could ever imagine.

In fact, Bill Gates dominated the market so thoroughly that the government had to step in and say, "Hey, slow down! You're too good at this." Think about that for a second. He was hauled into court because his success was so overwhelming that they accused him of forming a monopoly. They basically said, "You're so dominant, there's no room for anyone else to even compete."

This level of dominance isn't about luck or being in the right place at the right time—it's about understanding your value, executing relentlessly, and not stopping until you've claimed the market. Gates didn't just want to succeed; he wanted to own his lane so completely that even his competitors felt like they were playing a different game. That's what we're talking about here—the kind of success where there's no competition. The type of dominance where everyone else is just fighting for second place.

BE THE USAIN BOLT OF YOUR INDUSTRY

Speaking of dominating, let's talk about Usain Bolt for a minute. When Bolt stepped onto the track, nobody asked, "Is he going to win?"—they already knew the answer. The only question was, "Who's coming in second?" Usain Bolt was so dominant in his space that the other runners were literally competing to win silver and bronze medals.

That's the level of dominance we're aiming for. When you subdue your space, you're not just participating—you're setting the pace. You're the one everyone else is chasing. They're not competing with you—they're just trying to keep up. And that's the beauty of walking in your purpose. You're so in tune with your calling that everything flows effortlessly. The funny thing about Bolt is that he didn't just win; he made it look easy. That's what happens when you're operating in your proper lane —you're so good that it seems effortless.

But here's the thing about being like Bolt: it wasn't just natural talent. Sure, he was gifted, but his dominance came from work. Day in and day out, Bolt trained harder than anyone else. His ease on the track was the result of years of relentless preparation. Success at this level requires the same kind of dedication. It requires waking up daily and asking yourself, "Am I prepared to dominate my space today?" Because if you aren't, someone else is.

So, I ask you: Are you ready to be the Usain Bolt of your industry? To be the one everyone else is watching, wondering how you make it look so smooth? Remember, when you are prepared to put in the work behind the scenes, you'll naturally shine when it's time to perform.

FROM BILLS TO BUILDING

Let's get real for a second: Do you want to be stuck paying bills, or do you want to be like

Uncle Bill? Do you want to spend your life building someone else's dream, or do you want to make something of your own? You're either helping someone else get wealthy or creating wealth for yourself. You're either in the front of the line or standing on the sidelines, watching someone else dominate.

Think about it: while some people are content paying bills, true visionaries are focused on building legacies. Bill Gates, Jeff Bezos, Usain Bolt—they all started small. Gates and Bezos didn't have big corporate offices; they had garages. Bolt wasn't always a world record holder—he began as just another runner on a dirt track. The key is they didn't wait for perfect conditions. They didn't wait for a green light. They took action.

Greatness doesn't wait for permission—it demands it. So, while some folks are waiting for everything to line up perfectly, others are getting their hands dirty, building the foundation for something bigger than they ever imagined. Here's the reality: greatness starts small. You don't need millions of dollars or a big team. You need an idea, a drive, and the belief that you can fill a need no one else fills.

BE LIKE "THE B'S"

Let's break it down. How can you start dominating your space like Bill, Bolt, or Bezos? Here's the formula:

Find the Need and Fill It

Bill Gates saw a problem—computers needed an operating system. You need to find your problem. What is it that you can solve? What gap in the marketplace can you fill? The key to building wealth isn't just chasing money but solving problems. Ask yourself: What do people need, and how can I provide it?

Multiply What Works

It's not enough to have a great idea—you've got to reproduce it. Bill Gates didn't stop at one copy of Microsoft Windows. He put it in every single computer. What can you reproduce? How can you scale your product or service to reach more people?

Create a System for Replenishment

This is where the real wealth is made—replenishment. You need a system (like Bezos) that ensures your business, service, or idea can keep growing. Whether financial replenishment or restocking your products, build a machine that works even when you're not working. The goal is sustainability.

Dominate Like Bolt

Just like Usain Bolt didn't run races to place second, you're not here to merely participate. You're here to own your lane. Whether you're building a business, serving in your community, or developing a brand, your goal should be to subdue that space. Own it so thoroughly that when people think of your industry, they think of you.

FILL THAT BAG UP: FROM BILLS TO BILLIONS

So what's it going to be? Again, I ask, are you going to spend your life paying bills and living someone else's dream? Or will you be like Uncle Bill, building something that will fill your bag for generations to come? If you're tired of just scraping by and want to reach for something much bigger—if you're going to make the leap from paying bills to building billions—you already have everything you need to start. The seeds of greatness are already in you.

Let me tell you—no money has ever left this world. It hasn't disappeared; it hasn't been destroyed. It's still here, waiting to be claimed. The question is, will you get in line to collect, or will the line lead to you?

Here's the truth: It's all within your reach. You don't need permission. You don't need a million-dollar bank account. You need the willingness to start small and the courage to dominate once you've found your lane.

THE WORLD IS YOURS—GO GET IT

Every success story starts small. Bill Gates began in a garage, and Jeff Bezos packed books in his living room. Even Jesus started small, gathering a handful of disciples before His message spread like wildfire worldwide. They all started with humble beginnings, but they all ended up dominating their lanes and changing the world.

So what's it going to be? You've learned the steps. You've seen the blueprint. You know how to produce, how to multiply, how to replenish, subdue, and dominate. But now it's up to you.

If you want unlimited wealth, if you're going to build something that lasts, if you want to dominate in your space, then take the principles you've learned and apply them.

If not, it's cool. Go ahead and pass this book on to someone who is ready to achieve greatness. Who knows, you might build something together.

But I believe you're ready. The world is yours—and your lane is waiting for you to fill it. Fill that bag, build your empire, and leave your mark on the earth.

Les Brown once said, “Don’t just live your life; build something that lives on long after you’re gone.”

Pablo Picasso stated, “The meaning of life is to find your gift. The purpose of life is to give it away.”

Bruce Lee spoke these powerful words, “The key to immortality is first living a life worth remembering —and creating something worth leaving behind.”

I’m not a speaking legend like Les Brown, a world-renowned artist like Picasso, or a cultural icon like Bruce Lee, but here’s my own quote for you (actually, it's a series of questions).... Would you like to hear it? Here it goes!!!

> **"The question is not simply about paying bills or building billions. It’s about whether you will rise, awaken the power within, and take command of your destiny. Will you step out of the shadows and become the architect of a future so bold and transformative that it reshapes your life and the world for generations to come? Will you stand as a spectator, or will you claim your place among the legends who changed the course of history?”**

To be honest, I'm still trying to answer those questions, but I ask myself daily and will continue to move forward until I do.

Someday, I will "be" the answer… How about You?

Let's see what you can do!!!

ABOUT THE AUTHOR

Sidney Lloyd Robinson is an entrepreneur, author, and speaker, but more importantly, he's a proud father and Child/Man of God. In addition to that, Sidney hosts the weekly podcast Flawed Men of Faith, which focuses on equipping men of God to conquer the "Goliaths of life" through biblical yet practical tactics and strategies they can apply to their daily lives.

Prior to transitioning from employee to business owner and accepting his "creative calling," Sidney worked with industry titans JP Morgan Chase, Merrill Lynch, and Empower Retirement as a Banker, Registered Investment Broker and Advisor, and Certified Retirement Counselor.